WINTEGRITY

Win with Ethics, Trust, and Integrity

By Linda Swindling, JD, CSP

Wintegrity™

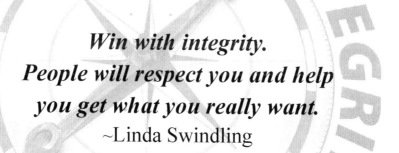

Win with integrity.
People will respect you and help
you get what you really want.
~Linda Swindling

CONTENTS

You are the creator of your character, the writer of your life's story, and the architect of your work life.

~Dianna Booher
Author of *Your Signature Life*

INTRODUCTION

Exhibiting ethics takes intention, discipline, and even courage. Daily choices of integrity build your ability to face even the toughest trials. Found in the word "integrity" is the word "grit." Choosing to do the right thing requires grit. Taking a stand against wrongdoing isn't always easy or popular.

Definition of Wintegrity

Wintegrity builds on the concept of interest-based negotiations and problem solving. You may already seek "win-win" outcomes and consider others' interests. Wintegrity expands the concept and intentionally includes the interests of all who may be affected, even those not present. The objective is to produce "win-win-win" results created with ethical practices supported by multiple people.

Wintegrity is:

- ➡ Acting in an ethical manner no matter what.
- ➡ Promoting the interests for all involved including your own.
- ➡ Making the best "right" decisions to build trust and respect.
- ➡ Creating solutions with the expectation that winning outcomes are possible for all involved.
- ➡ Considering resources involved and other stakeholders although they are not present or involved in the negotiation, deal, or transaction.

Use This Book as a Map

This book offers guidelines to help you chart your route to success. If you apply the tools and practices, you can steer clear of potential disasters and help negotiate the situations you encounter.

Think of this book as a map and your ethics as your compass. Just as you keep the needle heading towards true north, commit to doing what you know is right. On your journey pay close attention to your choices. Apply the principles of wintegrity to help you stay on course and reach your destination.

We all have within us our own Polaris, or True North, a fixed inner compass that we can look to for safe and reliable guidance when we feel we have lost our way.

~Anne Bruce, author of *Discover True North*

Navigating with wintegrity has a positive and lasting impact on your organization's culture, on your industry, and ultimately, on society. Whether you are an employee, a leader, a client, a parent, or a teenager, the principles and strategies can help you *win* in your personal and business relationships with *integrity.*

WINTEGRITY MEANS

WIN WITH INTEGRITY

MASTER ACTION PLAN

Answer these questions to reflect on your journey to date.

Up to this point in your life, whose guidance has helped you the most as you navigate right from wrong?

_____

_____

Where have you seen someone act in an ethical matter, even when no one is aware of the basis of the decision?

_____

_____

What bothers you the most when you think of unethical behavior?

_____

_____

Wintegrity Challenge

Based on your reading and responses above, complete this statement.

To improve my wintegrity journey, I commit to:

_____

_____

Here's what I think integrity is:
It's choosing courage over comfort.
Choosing what's right over what's
fun, fast or easy. And practicing
your values.

~Brené Brown

Author and Professor

1

INTEGRITY INSIDE

Fair dealings give you a competitive advantage. Have the tenacity and bravery to do what is right. When you act with integrity, you position yourself for possibilities that might exist.

Masters of Wintegrity

Masters of wintegrity have similar characteristics. Think of the most ethical people you know. What traits come to mind? Most likely they honor agreements. Their word is their bond. Deals can be done on a handshake. Daily, they stand up for what is right and good. They are resourceful, loyal, and dependable.

A Scout is trustworthy, loyal, helpful, friendly, courteous, kind, obedient, cheerful, thrifty, brave, clean, and reverent.

~Boy Scout Law

Wintegrity leaders are role models. They are open in personal and business dealings. They tell the truth and take appropriate action. In return, their people are loyal and provide higher performance.

According to a performance study found in *The Manager's High-Performance Handbook*, two-thirds of people report that they could focus and produce at least 25% more work if their leader took the following actions:

1. Provided regular and candid feedback.
2. Held others accountable to their commitments.
3. Acknowledged and gave them credit for their work.

You've got to give, give, give before you get, get, get.

~Joe Charbonneau, Hall of Fame speaker

Your Code

Professionals including doctors, lawyers, accountants, bankers, and architects have standards of ethics agreed upon by members in their field. These professionals have a large amount of discretion and usually a lesser degree of supervision.

Many trade associations and non-profit organizations require their members to follow ethical standards or principles to govern their conduct.

In your own work:

- Where could you face decisions involving integrity?
- Which areas in your control can impact others the most?
- When might someone in your position be tempted?

Walk Your Talk

A great way to earn respect is by living and practicing what you preach. This includes treating those around you with integrity.

Ask yourself these questions about your actions. Do you:

- ➤ Treat others both inside and outside your organization with fairness and respect?
- ➤ Provide quality goods and services to your customers in exchange for their hard-earned money?
- ➤ Demand adherence to high standards?
- ➤ Honor your promises and commitments?
- ➤ Avoid situations and people who are unethical?
- ➤ Communicate even when the news is not good?

Integrity is doing the right thing, even when no one is watching.

~ C. S. Lewis, author

Walking your talk adds to your credibility in your professional and personal relationships. Create your own professional and ethical standards before you are faced with a decision that requires them. When you ensure that honesty and fairness are part of your everyday behavior, you sleep better too.

WINTEGRITY MEANS

WALK YOUR TALK

MASTER ACTION PLAN

Answer these questions to support your integrity journey.

Consider people you admire for their integrity and credibility. What characteristics show that they "walk their talk"?

_____

_____

What one or two character traits could you strengthen to enhance your good reputation?

_____

_____

What does your personal code of ethics contain?

_____

_____

Wintegrity Challenge

Based on your reading and responses, complete this statement.

To improve my personal integrity journey, I commit to:

_____

_____

If you want to be proud of yourself,
you've got to DO things you can
be proud of. Feelings follow actions.

~Oselola McCarty
Former washer woman and the University
of Mississippi's most famous benefactor

DO UNTO OTHERS

Wintegrity is based on the premise that most people want to be a part of something bigger. They want their efforts to positively impact the world. Wintegrity also builds relationships because people feel respected and heard. Additionally, those who are dealt with honorably are less likely to renege on their agreements.

Stakeholders

Many people have a stake in your ethical and honorable behavior. Before implementing strategies or making decisions, think of whom your actions could affect and how those people might react. Your stakeholders may include:

- Customers and members.
- Employees and their families.
- Friends and family.
- Stockholders, owners, and boards.
- Government, governing bodies or the community.
- Vendors, suppliers, partners, and affiliates.

Make a list of people affected by your business decisions. When you associate names and faces as you choose a course of action, you find your choices are more personal and meaningful.

Be Nice

Every person deserves respect and courtesy. Talking down to others, especially those who help you, makes no sense. A receptionist, your wait staff, your dry cleaner, and a taxi driver deserve as much respect as a business owner or high-level executive. These hardworking people make the difference between a great experience and a bad one. Not only is being nice the right thing to do, you may be surprised by whom people know and the power they yield.

As someone who grew up in the Bronx, I certainly learned my share of four-letter words, but none are more powerful than nice.

~Linda Kaplan Thaler, author of *The Power of Nice*

Others' Contributions

If you want respect, concentrate on respecting others and the contributions they add. Being nice is a sign of strength, not weakness. While it may take longer, being nice when making a request usually gains you more trust, information, and commitment.

Help people feel at ease by:

- Acknowledging their experiences and perceptions.
- Considering words to say that show you mean them no harm.
- Listening. Genuinely consider their opinions or concerns.

Show your appreciation for others by thanking them specifically for the service or help they provide. Let them know how their effort or thoughtfulness benefits you or others. Thank their bosses for the aid you received and for allowing them to provide it. Write handwritten notes that recognize how meaningful their actions were. Call or visit to thank them in person. Be nice. Be grateful. Acknowledge others.

Good manners are for people who want to improve their people skills and to create relationships that bring more business.

~Colleen Rickenbacher, author of
Be on Your Best Business Behavior

Manners Matter

Good manners are important yet many people fail to use common courtesy. The advice seems so basic, yet few people do it. When you are polite, you show that you realize others are worthy of your respect. People will go the extra mile for someone who is simply considerate.

Why being polite pays off:

- Shows you are in control of your emotions.
- Gives an example of how you want to be treated.
- Words can't be used against you later.
- Pleasantly surprises others.
- Shows people you see them as people.
- Distinguishes you from others.
- Is a sign of good upbringing and class.

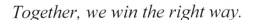

Together, we win the right way.

~Hewlett Packard Enterprises, employee value proposition

Create a Winning Work Environment

A lack of integrity and ethics may be most obvious at work when dealing with others. Often employees feel they are disrespected or have no control over their work environment. People who don't feel valued or respected find alternative ways to get their needs met. They complain to human resources, file claims with government entities, or take their talents to more appreciative employers.

Common courtesy and listening to others increases your chances for a positive result. One third of people are more likely to say "No" to a request if the person is inconsiderate or has bad manners.

Think back to a time when someone you trusted didn't honor you or refused to live up to a commitment. Remember the feeling of betrayal? Now consider your own actions. Have you:

- Told an ethnically or sexually-oriented joke?
- Gossiped or spread negative rumors?
- Bad mouthed the company or management?
- Passed along information shared in confidence?
- Withheld information that others needed?
- Taken credit for another's accomplishment?
- Failed to admit to or correct a mistake?

Like you, people want to be treated fairly and with dignity. Perception and communication play a big part in how people view their environment at home and at work.

Little Things Add Up

Seemingly insignificant actions can create the biggest integrity erosions. These small acts also provide the greatest opportunities for improvement. Examine how you:

- Handle little white lies.
- Treat and talk about co-workers.
- Write e-mails or use social media.
- Document billing, time, estimates, costs, and expenses.
- Make, keep, or avoid commitments.
- Treat "unimportant" work rules.
- Share credit with others.

When you feel the desire to hide the truth, take the time to jot down what you will actually gain and what you could lose.

~Eric Harvey, President of
The Walk the Talk Company

WINTEGRITY MEANS

TREAT OTHERS THE BEST POSSIBLE WAY

MASTER ACTION PLAN

*Answer these questions to support your journey of
treating others with respect and integrity.*

Who could you help that you aren't required to help? How?

_____

_____

How can you show gratitude to one person each day this week? Be
specific in recognizing how he/she helped.

_____

_____

What mistake or miscommunication can you correct? How can you
respectfully apologize to the person/people affected?

_____

_____

Wintegrity Challenge

Based on your reading and responses, complete this statement.

To improve how I respect and treat others, I commit to:

_____

_____

Honesty is the cornerstone of all success, without which confidence and ability to perform shall cease to exist.

~Mary Kay Ash
Founder, Mary Kay Cosmetics, Inc.

ETHICS EXAM

Acting with wintegrity means constantly thinking about your next steps. You concentrate on ensuring your actions are ethical, are honest, meet your personal standards, and are acceptable to others.

Test Your Decisions

Before acting, "test" your decisions by asking these questions:

- ➤ Is it legal?
- ➤ Does my decision comply with company rules and guidelines?
- ➤ Am I in sync with the organizational mission and values?
- ➤ Will I be comfortable and guilt-free if I do it?
- ➤ Does it match our stated commitments and guarantees?
- ➤ Would I act this way with my family or friends?
- ➤ Would I mind if someone behaved this way with me?
- ➤ Would the most ethical person I know do it?

Commit to taking total responsibility for everything that happens to you. This one change in thinking has the power to launch you to the world-class level faster than any other single idea.

~Steve Siebold, author of *How Rich People Think*

Unacceptable and Non-Negotiable

Understanding what behavior falls into the unacceptable category is critical. Common practices in certain industries or organizations may be taboo in your industry or company. For instance, paying a referral fee is common practice in many businesses. However, attorneys can't pay referral fees to people who aren't attorneys.

Certain industries regulate their members' behavior. What might be considered legal may also be considered unethical or out of compliance for that profession. Just as families and communities have different cultures and norms, varying operational guidelines exist in different organizations. Similarly, behavior may not comply with a certain company's or association's culture or beliefs.

Don't ask 'What can I get away with?' Ask, 'What's the right thing to do?'

~Russ Riddle, author of *Lawyer Up the Smart Way*

Discrimination is illogical and should not be tolerated. Everyone wants respect, appreciation, and to work in a safe environment.

Zero Tolerance

Most organizations have zero tolerance for the:

- → Violation of laws and regulations.
- → Harassment of employees or those reporting violations.
- → Disclosure of trade secrets.
- → Critical health and safety concerns.
- → Violence against others.

Would you treat those items like that if you owned them? I raised you better than that. Show respect for other people and their property.

~Mom

Mirror Test

Self-evaluation is a critical component of business ethics. Periodically examining one's behavior takes courage. Reflect over the last several months. Have you:

- → Conducted personal business on company time?
- → Used resources for personal purposes?
- → Called in sick when you weren't?
- → Ignored or violated a rule or procedure?
- → Failed to follow through on a promise?
- → Knowingly delivered poor quality?
- → Been less than honest or manipulated the truth?
- → Accepted an inappropriate gift or gratuity?

WINTEGRITY MEANS
COMMIT TO HIGH STANDARDS

MASTER ACTION PLAN

Answer these questions to support your ethical journey.

What questions could you apply to the next big decision you face?

_____

_____

What changes would improve your ethical reflection in the mirror? How will you make those changes?

_____

_____

What measures do you have in place to protect you and those around you against unacceptable behavior?

_____

_____

Wintegrity Challenge

Based on your reading and responses, complete this statement.

To improve my ethical journey, I commit to:

_____

_____

When people show you who they are, believe them (the first time).
~Maya Angelou
Author and Civil Rights Activist

SHOW RESPECT

Respect applies to people, resources, and environments. When people don't feel valued or respected, their drive decreases to accept responsibility or improve performance.

Take Responsibility

Wintegrity means taking responsibility for:

- ➡ Treating customers, co-workers, and vendors with dignity.
- ➡ Using supplies, equipment, time, and money appropriately, efficiently, and for the business only.
- ➡ Protecting your work environment.
- ➡ Abiding by all rules and regulations.
- ➡ Working collaboratively and sharing the load.
- ➡ Meeting performance expectations and adding value.

You may have legitimate reasons or explanations why you made a different choice or could not follow through on a promise. If so, communicate your reasons early on. Avoid excuses. As a leader, use communication to eliminate the "ignorance of the rules" excuse.

Overuse of the phrase "It is not my job" can quickly lead to not having a job.

Excuse Makers

Smart professionals avoid those who excuse unethical behavior. Some rationalizations for choosing not to act with integrity are:

> "Everyone else (my boss) does it."
> "They'll never miss it."
> "They owe it to me."
> "No one will know or care."
> "They won't ever read this."
> "I don't have time to do it right."
> "That's close enough."
> "Some rules were meant to be broken."
> "It's not my job."

If you don't have time to do it right, when will you have time to fix it?

~Dad

Out of Integrity

Not living in integrity can cause stress, loss of sleep, and even physical or mental problems. Despite the ill effects, people have all sorts of justifications of why they choose to follow an unethical path or break the rules. Here are a few:

- ➡ Acquiring more and more with disregard to others' needs.
- ➡ Cutting corners to keep up.
- ➡ Taking the path of least resistance.

- Acting or reacting without thinking.
- Competing or yielding to peer pressure.
- Worrying or concerns over losing one's job.
- Wanting to perform or please others.
- Not wanting to look stupid or unknowledgeable.

78% of people report spending a minimum of 3-6 hours a week dealing with negative people and the situations they cause.

Avoid Negativity

Negativity can result when one is stressed, especially when someone's actions are incongruent with his or her beliefs or values. Negativity is counterproductive. It erodes trust and integrity and can even foster unethical and illegal acts.

Avoid people who:

- Say things like "It will never work."
- Openly criticize the organization.
- Insult their boss or leadership.
- Hide the truth or a mistake.
- Reassign blame and shirk responsibility.
- Exclude others or spread rumors.
- Don't keep confidences.
- Moan, complain, and drag others down.

WINTEGRITY MEANS

RESPECT PEOPLE AND RESOURCES

MASTER ACTION PLAN

Answer these questions to support your respect journey.

What would help others feel respected and/or more at ease?
How could you assist?

_____

_____

What stressors cause you to complain or become negative?

_____

_____

How can you avoid making excuses or complaining for a week?

_____

_____

Wintegrity Challenge

Based on your reading and responses, complete this statement.

To improve my journey towards respect, I commit to:

_____

_____

It is better to light a candle than curse the darkness.

~Eleanor Roosevelt
Former First Lady of the United States

FISHBOWL LEADERSHIP

To a large degree, leaders operate in a fishbowl. Employees are constantly watching their actions. They listen to what their leaders say and then compare those words to actions.

Model Ethical Behavior

Wintegrity leaders model ethical behavior. They strive to:

- ➡ Reduce pressure to compromise standards.
- ➡ Increase early detection of misconduct.
- ➡ Improve trust and respect at all levels.
- ➡ Increase pride, professionalism, and productivity.
- ➡ Protect a positive culture and reputation.
- ➡ Attract and retain talented, diverse employees.

If you are a leader, review your compensation plans, internal policies, and procedures to ensure that employees aren't encouraged to "game" the system to improve rankings, numbers, or compensation. Communicating well helps minimize excuses for "ignorance of the rules" and reduces the risk of unethical actions.

Be about what the business says it is about.

~David Cottrell, author of
Monday Morning Motivation

Mission Possible

One indicator that an organization is ethical is competent job performance. Quality effort directly equates to quality products and services. The top three ways to get teams to work successfully towards a common goal are to provide:

1. Clear directions and holding people accountable.
2. Communication of strategy from leadership.
3. A high level of trust.

If you are in a leadership role, help others reach their best by:

- Sharing job requirements, expectations, and progress.
- Copying and updating others on guidelines and laws.
- Providing information about the organization, customers, products, services, and the industry.
- Supporting and giving clear direction from management.
- Granting permission to make mistakes.
- Communicating strategy and relating it to their role.
- Allowing a way to report violations without retribution.
- Responding quickly and thoroughly to unethical and/or inappropriate behaviors or activities

Fair and Respectful

Relationships built on fairness and respect benefit all involved. When you are honest and creative in your attempts to find a "fair" solution, you may be surprised at the positive reactions you receive.

Often, people who trust you reveal opportunities you weren't aware were available. Ask questions to find others' true interests before you make a request based on yours. People who receive polite requests and considerate treatment often feel a need to reciprocate.

The reciprocity rule says that we should try to repay, in kind, what another person has provided us.

~Robert B. Cialdini, author of *Influence:
The Psychology of Persuasion and Pre-suasion*

Involve Others

Building a culture of respect takes more than one person. Wintegrity leaders share what they *expect* and then *inspect* the outcomes. They:

- Recognize others' efforts and behavior.
- Expect and allow for mistakes.
- Practice patience, understanding, and empathy.
- Talk *with* people, not *at* them or *about* them.
- Are polite and go the extra mile.
- Commit to ongoing self-development.
- Listen as much as they speak.
- Apologize for mistakes.
- Tell others when they feel slighted.
- Welcome constructive feedback and ideas.
- Guard secrets and protect sensitive information.
- Use ethics and performance in promoting or hiring.
- Comment on integrity in feedback and reviews.

WINTEGRITY MEANS

MODEL THE BEHAVIOR YOU WANT

MASTER ACTION PLAN

Answer these questions to support your leadership journey.

To whom do you go for advice when you are unsure or in doubt?

_____

_____

What do you say when someone makes mistakes on work that affects you?

_____

_____

Where can you do a better job involving others?

_____

_____

Wintegrity Challenge

Based on your reading and responses, complete this statement.

To improve my leadership journey, I commit to:

_____

_____

While it may appear to be static, trust is more like a forest – a long time growing, but easily burned down with a touch of carelessness.

~David Horsager
Author of *The Trust Edge*

TRUST FACTOR

A few people have a higher "trust factor" built into their demeanor. These lucky people possess the ability to connect quickly and make a trustworthy first impression. Some people put others at ease with their presence alone. What a gift to walk into a room and know people perceive you as honest, respectable, and approachable.

Low Trust Consequences

Have you experienced the uncomfortable position where your intentions or character are questioned? Were your words misunderstood, or comments interpreted the wrong way? Maybe your sarcasm or jokes are a welcome distraction for most but are perceived as hurtful remarks by others. Perhaps due to circumstances out of your control, a person doesn't trust you.

35% of people will deny a request or tell others "no" when they don't like or trust them.

Low trust hurts relationships. People stop confiding in you or begin avoiding you. At work, you are micromanaged. At home, your loved ones withdraw. To regain trust, refocus your efforts to communicate, apologize if needed, and honor your promises.

Never compromise what's right and uphold your family name. You've got to stand for something or you'll fall for anything.

~Aaron Tippin, lyrics from song *You've Got to Stand for Something*

Wintegrity Rules for Teams

Experts who facilitate, mediate, and moderate difficult discussions know the secret to managing meetings. They ask participants to define desired outcomes and behaviors *before* discussions begin. Following "rules of engagement" increases courtesy and respect, especially when topics get heated. People who agree to basic rules of conduct are more likely to honor and to monitor their behavior.

Sample rules of engagement for meeting management include:

- Start on time and follow an agenda to honor others' time.
- Make sure everyone has a voice and is participating instead of a few members dominating conversations.
- Agree about electronic devices. (Ex. All on? Off? Silent?).
- Determine confidentiality and what can be communicated.
- Address each idea by deciding to do it, dump it or delay it.
- Ensure goals are S.M.A.R.T. (Specific, Measurable, Achievable, Relevant, Time-bound with fixed due dates).

WINTEGRITY MEANS

CREATE AND FOLLOW TEAM RULES

MASTER ACTION PLAN

Answer these questions to support your trust journey.

Watch someone with the "trust factor". What behaviors and words do they use?

_____

_____

What rules can you and your team create to improve your meetings?

_____

_____

How could you build trust with two people this week?

_____

_____

Wintegrity Challenge

Based on your reading and responses, complete this statement.

To improve my trust journey, I commit to:

_____

_____

We each have a responsibility in business to simply do what is right and police ourselves. Yes, honesty is not always easy or fun. It isn't the best policy. It is the only policy.

~Howard Putnam
The Winds of Turbulence and Former
CEO of Southwest and Braniff Airlines

Do the Right Thing

Organizations practice wintegrity when they responsibly consider how their actions impact the community and/or world. They choose to do the "right" things and avoid compromising positions. When unsure, their people ask for guidance. Teams with ethical business practices are often more profitable. They attract and retain talent.

When in Doubt Ask

An objective viewpoint is invaluable in deciding what is right when there are no apparent wrongs. Smart professionals seek assistance and keep asking until they get answers. They establish relationships before they need them. Wise counsel may be:

- An owner, boss, manager, or team lead.
- A trusted advisor, mentor or executive coach.
- An industry expert or seasoned professional.
- A human resource professional.
- A counselor or clergy.
- A member of the legal team, ethics department or hotline.

Just Say No

Some actions are best to avoid. When you are faced with a potentially unethical situation, you need phrases to say "no" or "opt out" and still maintain the relationship. Try these:

"Let's check this out with (a higher authority) before we act."
"That's not going to work for me."
"That might be considered unethical."
"There has got to be a more ethical approach to this."
"Why don't we try another solution instead?"
"No thanks. I'm going to pass."

Choosing Between Two Right Answers

A potential ethical dilemma happens when one has to choose between two options which are both correct. For instance, it is:

Right to...	And *Also* Right to...
Apply rules and procedures equally, without favoritism.	Give special consideration to hard working, dependable, and productive employees.
Keep information given to you in confidence.	Report violations of laws, rules, and ethical standards.
Tell the truth. Be candid and forthcoming.	Be tactful and considerate of peoples' feelings and emotions.
Be concerned with short-term results and immediate issues.	Focus on long-term growth and stability.

So be sure when you step,
Step with care and great tact.
And remember that life's
A Great Balancing Act.

~Dr. Seuss, author of *Oh, the Places You'll Go*

More Right

When identifying and choosing between two seemingly right decisions, it helps to look at common criteria or questions. When faced with tough choices that all appear to have merit, try asking what decision:

- ➤ Is most in line with laws, regulations, and corporate procedures?
- ➤ Is most in sync with organizational values?
- ➤ Provides the greatest benefit for the largest number of stakeholders?
- ➤ Establishes the best precedent for guiding similar decisions in the future?
- ➤ Is not something that we could regret in the future?

Remind yourself and others that the only dumb question is the one that was not asked.

Decisions that Benefit

Social consciousness or social responsibility involves thinking beyond the people directly involved in an opportunity or deal. Companies are finding the more they invest in the community, the more customers and employees invest in them. They are transparent and conduct their business "in the open." Wintegrity organizations are profitable, attract and retain employees, and look at business as a means to impact the world.

Our restaurant business is fed by the interest of our community in us and so as we become known for our genuine interest in them, our business grows organically.

~Tim McCarthy, owner of 20 Raising Cane's restaurants and Chief Mission Officer of The Business of Good Foundation

Wintegrity means working with ethics and integrity to promote winning results for you and others involved. Wintegrity leaders agree with the philosophy that doing the right thing is everyone's responsibility. These leaders exhibit business ethics with intention, discipline, and courage. Wintegrity positively impacts others, the world, and all aspects of your life!

WINTEGRITY MEANS

CONSIDER YOUR IMPACT ON THE WORLD

MASTER ACTION PLAN

Answer these questions to support your journey to do the right thing.

What one decision could you take to a trusted advisor for advice?

_____

_____

How have you tactfully handled a potentially unethical situation?

_____

_____

Identify one project that could be structured to also give back
to the community or non-profit. How can you make it happen?

_____

_____

Wintegrity Challenge

Based on your reading and responses, complete this statement.

To continue my efforts to do more of what's right, I commit to:

_____

_____

WINTEGRITY MEANS

WIN WITH INTEGRITY

WALK YOUR TALK

TREAT OTHERS THE BEST POSSIBLE WAY

COMMIT TO HIGH STANDARDS

RESPECT PEOPLE AND RESOURCES

CREATE AND FOLLOW TEAM RULES

MODEL THE BEHAVIOR YOU WANT

CONSIDER YOUR IMPACT ON THE WORLD

MASTER ACTION PLAN

Based on your reading, reflection, and responses:

What will you do more of?

_____

_____

What will you do less of?

_____

_____

What will you do more effectively?

_____

_____

Plot your course with high standards. Go seek ethical solutions that benefit all involved. Pay great attention to trust and honesty. Help others win and accomplish their goals with integrity. Make a positive impact on the world. May all your relationships and adventures be filled with wintegrity!

Journey On with Wintegrity!

A Note of Thanks

This book would not have been possible without Eric Harvey, president of *The Walk the Talk Company.* Eric published *The Manager's High-Performance Handbook* and co-authored the *Passport to Success* series book on ethics, *Do the Right Thing.* Thank you, Zan Jones. Without your guidance, this book wouldn't have come to fruition. Tim Cocklin, thanks for your creativity with this book. And thank you to my family, friends, clients, and readers.

Resources

Statistics, data, and rankings found in this book are derived from research conducted in conjunction with the following books, also authored by Linda Byars Swindling, JD, CSP.

Ask Outrageously!
The Secret to Getting What You Really Want
Asking outrageously does not mean being obnoxious or taking advantage of others. It means making a bold ask to reach amazing outcomes…just by asking.

The Manager's High-Performance Handbook
How to Drive Winning Performance with Everyone on Your Team
On a high-performance team everyone is committed to a common purpose. Members are trusting, innovative, and collaborative. They provide superior results and gain winning outcomes.

Stop Complainers & Energy Drainers:
How to Negotiate Work Drama to Get More Done
Constant complainers take up resources, time, and mental bandwidth in the workplace. When you change a culture of complainers to one of contributors, you boost morale and get more done with less drama.

How to Order this Book

To order additional copies of this book visit Amazon.com.

For quantity discounts of 100 books or more, please email
info@LindaSwindling.com or call (972) 416-3652.

**Books and additional resources can be found at
LindaSwindling.com.**

About the Author

From the courtroom to the boardroom, Linda Byars Swindling, JD, CSP, knows firsthand about ethical communication and influencing decision makers. Her specialty is helping people communicate powerfully so others will listen. Linda is the owner of Journey On, a speaking and professional development firm. She is an experienced consultant, keynote speaker, executive coach, master facilitator, and a TEDxSMU presenter.

How Can I Work with Linda?

Linda works with organizations that want to realize appreciable results in the areas of negotiation, communication, sales, team effectiveness, high performance, and leadership. Her interactive style focuses on achieving goals, finding solutions, increasing profitability, and strategically gaining support and influence.

Ask Linda to Keynote Your Next Conference

Her most popular speeches are:

- Ask Outrageously! The Secret to Getting What You Really Want
- Positively Negotiate Work Drama
- High-Performance Secrets for High-Stakes Results
- Wintegrity: You Don't Have to Be a Jerk to Get Deals that Work

Ask Linda to Emcee or Moderate Your Event

Ask Linda to Facilitate Your Strategic or Leadership Meeting

Ask Linda to Help You Grow Your Leaders

LindaSwindling.com

44485775R00033

Made in the USA
Middletown, DE
07 May 2019